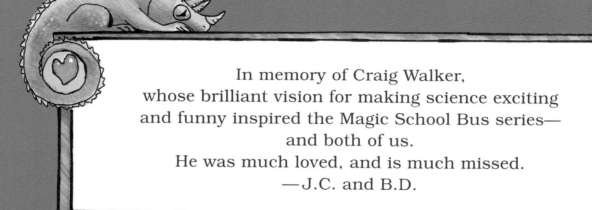

In memory of Craig Walker,
whose brilliant vision for making science exciting
and funny inspired the Magic School Bus series—
and both of us.
He was much loved, and is much missed.
—J.C. and B.D.

The Magic School Bus
and the Climate Challenge

The Magic School Bus

and the Climate Challenge

By Joanna Cole
Illustrated by Bruce Degen

RECYCLED PAPER

Scholastic Inc.
New York   Toronto   London   Auckland
Sydney   Mexico City   New Delhi   Hong Kong

Many have helped in the making of this book. In particular, our sincere thanks go to

Dr. Bill Chameides, Dean and Nicholas Professor of the Environment, Duke University,

for his enthusiastic and informed review.

Library of Congress Cataloging-in-Publication Data is available

ISBN 978-0-545-45377-6

Text copyright © 2010 by Joanna Cole.
Illustrations copyright © 2010 by Bruce Degen.
All rights reserved. Published by Scholastic Press,
an imprint of Scholastic Inc., *Publishers since 1920*.
SCHOLASTIC, THE MAGIC SCHOOL BUS, and associated
logos are trademarks and/or registered trademarks of Scholastic Inc.

12 11 10 9 8 7 6 5 4 3 2 1   12 13 14 15 16/0
Printed in China   95

This edition first printing, April 2012

The text type was set in Bookman Light.
The illustrator used pen and ink, watercolor, color pencil, and gouache for the paintings in this book.

To all our friends in Korea.
We will never forget your warm and enthusiastic
welcome to The Magic School Bus, and to us.
— J.C. and B.D.

WELCOME, JOON

OUR VISITOR FROM
SOUTH KOREA

ANIMALS OF THE ARCTIC

POLAR BEARS
by Tim

WHALE by Keesha

SEALS
by Ralphie

WALRUS by Carlos

Have you heard about our teacher, Ms. Frizzle? Almost every day, something weird happens in her class.

IN CASE YOU DIDN'T NOTICE, MS. FRIZZLE IS THE STRANGEST TEACHER IN SCHOOL.

I NOTICED, I NOTICED!

ARCTIC HARE
by Arnold

ARCTIC OWL
by Wanda

ARCTIC FOX
by Phoebe

JOON

OUR WONDERFUL WORLD

MOSS

LICHENS

For example, take the day we started to study global warming. We were going to put on a play about Earth and all the changes that are happening.

The Friz had brought a book from home, and we were using the pictures to help us paint the scenery.

WHAT IS GLOBAL WARMING?
by Carlos

Global warming is a rise in the average temperature of the land and water on Earth. Today, the average temperature is more than 1 degree F warmer than it was 100 years ago.

One degree doesn't sound like much, but one small degree has caused big changes already— ice melting, seas rising, and more freak weather!

"Ms. Frizzle's book is kind of old," said Tim. "It came out before things really started heating up."
"I'll go online to get new pictures," said Wanda. She headed for a computer, but Ms. Frizzle was already out the door. "Come on, class," she called. "Bring my book, please."

LET'S GET REALLY UP-TO-DATE INFORMATION.

I HATE IT WHEN SHE SAYS STUFF LIKE THAT.

WELL, I'VE HEARD HER NAME IS VALERIE....

BUT I CAN'T BELIEVE SHE WAS EVER NINE!

LET'S GO!

OUR WONDERFUL WORLD

This book belongs to Valerie Frizzle age 9.

Before you could say "North Pole,"
the Friz herded us onto the bus.
She pushed a few buttons and pulled a few levers.
Then we were on our way to the Arctic Sea—
a place with a completely different climate.

When we got there, Dorothy Ann opened
Ms. Frizzle's old book.
The pictures showed ice everywhere.
There was still plenty of ice in the Arctic,
but a lot had melted, and more
was melting all the time.

MELTING CAUSES MORE MELTING
by Tim

Ice is white. White reflects most of the sunlight that hits it. So the sun can't heat up the ice.

Water is not white. It absorbs most of the sunlight that hits it. So the water gets warmer.

SUN

ICE REFLECTS

WATER ABSORBS

IN THE ARCTIC, AN AREA HAS MELTED THAT'S THE SIZE OF TEXAS AND CALIFORNIA COMBINED!

HOW IT LOOKS NOW

This starts a dangerous loop:
- The warm water melts more ice.
- That means there is more water.
- This water takes in more sunlight.
- So the water gets warmer and melts even more ice.

And so on, and so on, until all the ice is gone.

CALIFORNIA

TEXAS

Ms. Frizzle steered the bus-plane
all over the earth.
We saw changes everywhere.

5. Warming causes stronger hurricanes and tornadoes...

...and more forest fires...

...and bigger blizzards.

GLOBAL WARMING PUTS MORE WATER IN THE AIR IN SOME PLACES. THAT MEANS MORE RAIN, AND, WHEN IT GETS COLD, MORE SNOW!

WHY IS THERE STILL COLD WEATHER?
by Keesha.
Global warming means that the average temperature of the whole earth is rising.
Different places still have different weather, but, in most places, there are more hot days and fewer cold days than before.

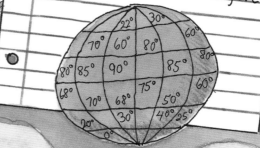

6. It causes animals and plants to die or to move.

IT'S TOO HOT HERE.

LET'S GO NORTH.

YELLOW-BELLIED MARMOTS

FIRE ANTS

7. Strange weather hurts food crops.

ICE ON AVOCADOS

THAT WHOLE CROP MIGHT BE LOST!

NO AVOCADOS? HOLY GUACAMOLE!

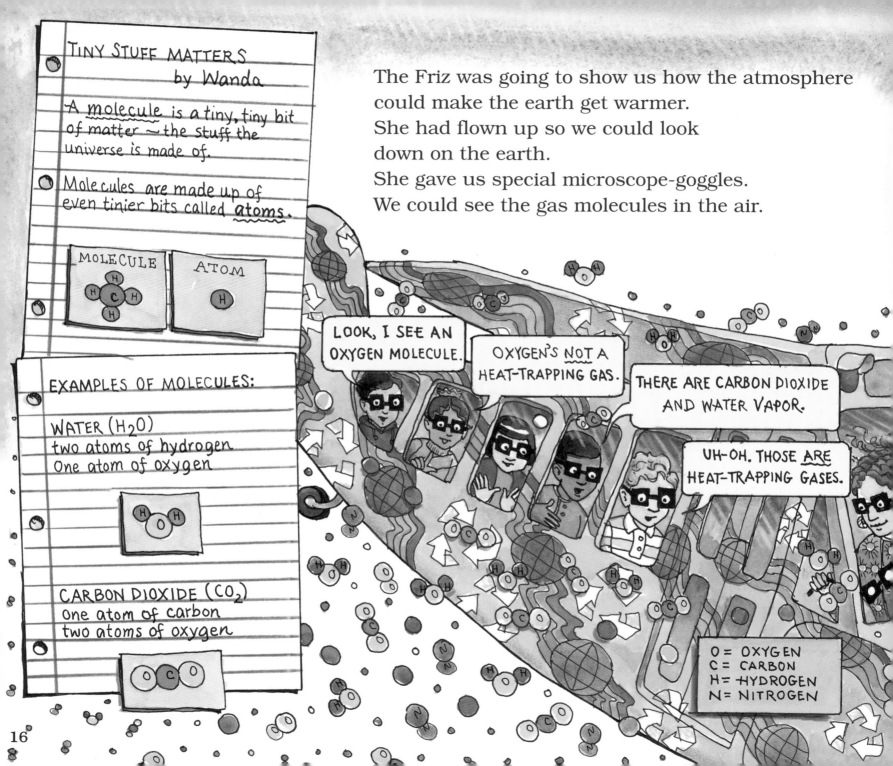

The Friz was going to show us how the atmosphere could make the earth get warmer.
She had flown up so we could look down on the earth.
She gave us special microscope-goggles.
We could see the gas molecules in the air.

The greenhouse gases trapped some of the heat. That heat headed back to Earth again. It raised the earth's temperature even higher than before.

WE'RE GOING DOWN TO EARTH AGAIN!

WE'RE BEING FRIZZLED AGAIN!

IS THE GREENHOUSE EFFECT BAD?
by Carlos

The greenhouse effect isn't all bad. If there weren't any heat-trapping gases the earth would freeze up.

The natural greenhouse effect keeps the earth at the right temperature for us.

THANK GOODNESS FOR THE NATURAL GREENHOUSE EFFECT!

But when there are too many greenhouse gases, the earth heats up too much. This causes trouble!

I AM ONE HOT DOG!

19

Wow! We had finally found out what was causing climate change. It was mostly people—including us. We panicked!

MOST OF THAT CO₂ IS BEING MADE BY THINGS PEOPLE DO!

AND THE CO₂ IS MAKING THE EARTH WARMER AND WARMER!

Q: WHY DO PEOPLE BURN FOSSIL FUELS?

A: TO MAKE ENERGY
by Carlos

Energy is the power to do work.

People need energy to:
• heat houses
• cook food
• run vehicles
• run machines
• make light

Our teacher shooed us back on the bus-plane. Like it or not, we were on our way to see some alternative energy.

IF THE FRIZ IS GOING, WE HAVE TO GO, TOO.

WE DON'T HAVE AN ALTERNATIVE.

ALL ABOARD

TONS OF CO₂
by Keesha

Q: How much CO_2 goes into the atmosphere for each person in the U.S.?

A: Too much!
About 44,000 pounds a year. That's the same as eight hefty hippos per person every year!

REDUCING CO₂ ~ WHAT'S OUR GOAL?

By the year 2050, Americans should have reduced their hippos a lot. Instead of eight hippos, an American should emit less than one hippo per year.

23

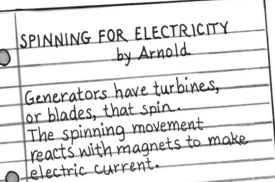

SPINNING FOR ELECTRICITY
by Arnold

Generators have turbines, or blades, that spin. The spinning movement reacts with magnets to make electric current.

We set out to see generators—
machines that make electricity.
Most generators burn fossil fuel to spin
their turbines and make electricity.
Alternative generators make it without fossil fuels.

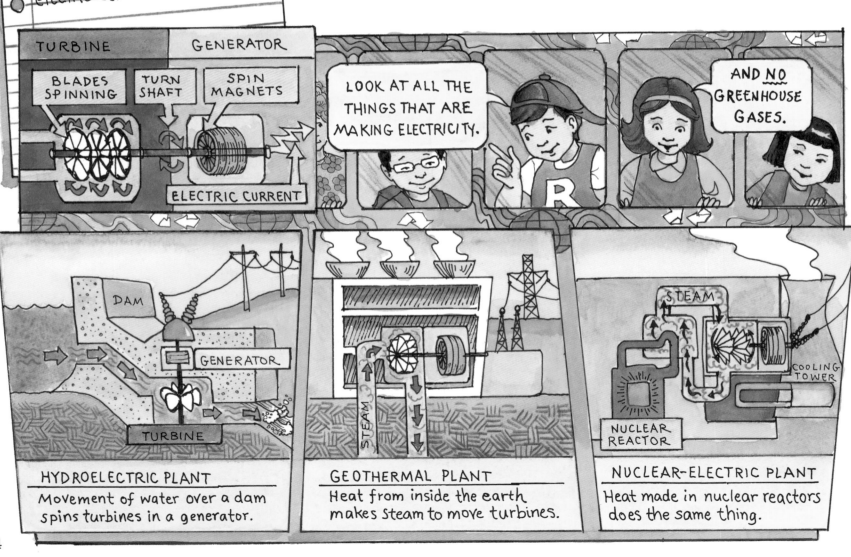

TURBINE | GENERATOR

BLADES SPINNING → TURN SHAFT → SPIN MAGNETS

ELECTRIC CURRENT

LOOK AT ALL THE THINGS THAT ARE MAKING ELECTRICITY.

AND NO GREENHOUSE GASES.

HYDROELECTRIC PLANT
Movement of water over a dam spins turbines in a generator.

GEOTHERMAL PLANT
Heat from inside the earth makes steam to move turbines.

NUCLEAR-ELECTRIC PLANT
Heat made in nuclear reactors does the same thing.

24

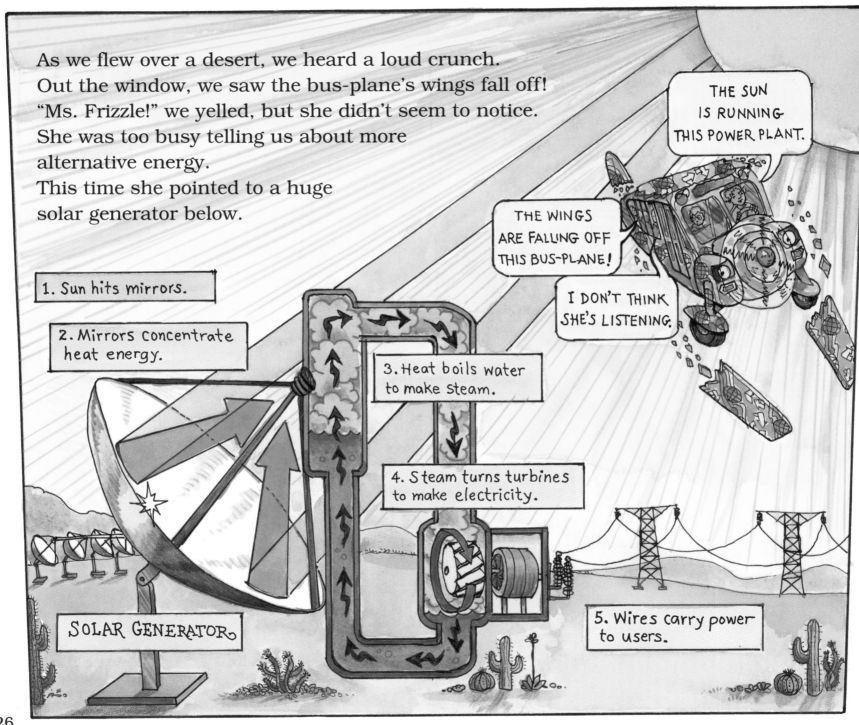

The bus made a crash landing.
Oops, we mean a *splash* landing.
We were floating in a solar-heated swimming pool.
Ms. Frizzle kept talking, telling us about solar cells.
They make energy directly from the sun—
with no moving parts.

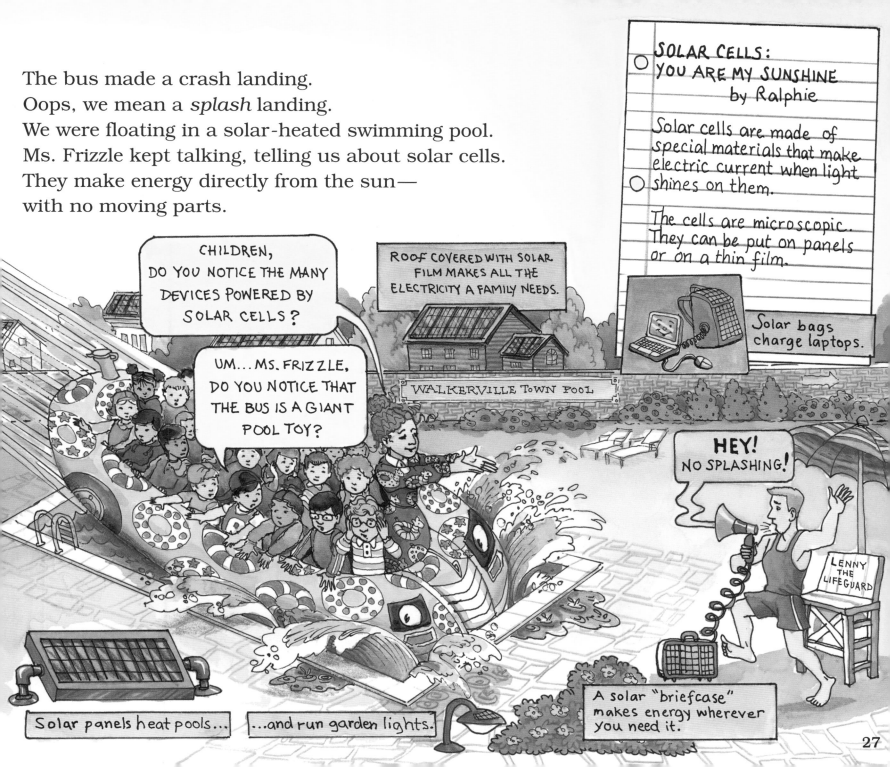

SOLAR CELLS:
YOU ARE MY SUNSHINE
by Ralphie

Solar cells are made of special materials that make electric current when light shines on them.

The cells are microscopic. They can be put on panels or on a thin film.

Solar bags charge laptops.

CHILDREN, DO YOU NOTICE THE MANY DEVICES POWERED BY SOLAR CELLS?

ROOF COVERED WITH SOLAR FILM MAKES ALL THE ELECTRICITY A FAMILY NEEDS.

UM...MS. FRIZZLE, DO YOU NOTICE THAT THE BUS IS A GIANT POOL TOY?

WALKERVILLE TOWN POOL

HEY! NO SPLASHING!

LENNY THE LIFEGUARD

Solar panels heat pools...

...and run garden lights.

A solar "briefcase" makes energy wherever you need it.

27

The bus stopped being a pool toy, so we rode into town. Everywhere, people were saving energy. Instead of driving private cars, many were using trains, buses, taxis, and bikes, as well as more fuel-efficient vehicles.

Ms. Frizzle pulled a bright green lever. At once the bus morphed into a hybrid vehicle that ran on gasoline and a rechargeable battery.
"Can we please go back to school, Ms. Frizzle?" we begged. "We've been on this bus too long!"
For once our teacher listened.

MORE WORDS FROM DOROTHY ANN

A HYBRID VEHICLE uses more than one source of energy.

A FUEL-EFFICIENT vehicle uses **less** fuel to go **more** miles.

KIDS CAN...
Take the school bus instead of being driven by a parent.

EVEN AN INEFFICIENT SCHOOL BUS EMITS LESS CO_2 THAN 20 CARS DRIVING KIDS TO SCHOOL.

KIDS CAN... Ask adults to stop letting vehicles idle.

PLEASE TURN OFF YOUR ENGINE WHILE WAITING.

We had to start saving energy right away.
"Conserve, conserve, conserve!" shouted the Friz.
"Recycle, recycle, recycle!"

MORE WORDS FROM D.A.

Conserve means to avoid waste.

Recycle means to treat waste materials so they can be used again.

RECYCLING SAVES ENERGY
by Tim

Making new cans from recycled cans uses 30% less energy than making them from new aluminum.

KIDS CAN...
Recycle cans and bottles!

A LITTLE CAN DO A LOT
If your town recycled 2,000 pounds of aluminum cans, it would save enough energy to heat the typical home for 10 years.

31

We started making changes at our school.
There was plenty of room for improvement.
Then we called the mayor of our town.
Then we wrote to the president.

We told everyone, "Let's cut down on greenhouse gases now!"

❖ Don't leave the fridge open too long.
❖ Buy Energy Star appliances.

IT'S NOT COOL TO LEAVE THE FRIDGE OPEN!

ENERGY STAR

❖ Buy things with less packaging.
❖ Buying MORE local produce...

...SAVES ON PACKAGING AND TRANSPORTATION.

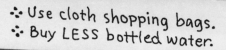

❖ Use cloth shopping bags.
❖ Buy LESS bottled water.

❖ Air-dry your laundry.

A LITTLE CAN DO A LOT

If every household in the U.S. switched three lights to compact fluorescent lamps (CFLS), it would reduce as much CO_2 as taking 3.5 million cars off the road.

That's because old incandescent bulbs waste a lot of energy making heat. CFLS use most of their energy making light.

THE LESS ENERGY YOU USE, THE LESS CO_2 GOES INTO THE AIR.

Finally, we had time to put on our play.
It was about everything we had seen on our trip.
We showed what global warming was doing to our planet.
And we told about how people can help.

QUESTIONS FOR MS. FRIZZLE'S CLASS
... an online chat

Q. Can a class really go up in the sky and ride sunbeams into the earth?
from IvannaNO@once.now

A. According to our research, only Ms. Frizzle's class can do that.
from Dorothy.Ann@a.loss.to.explain.net

Q. Why are you so worried about global warming? There were warm times in Earth's past, weren't there?
from Onceupon@time.now

A. In past times, Earth's climate has been cool, cold, warm, and hot. But these changes have happened over millions of years. Animals and plants had time to adjust. The warming we see now has happened in only a few hundred years. We can't adapt that fast.
from Ralphie@a.gallop.net

Q. Can a single person really change things?
from <u>Juan@atime4change.net</u>

A. One individual can't make a big difference.
But millions of individuals can!
from <u>Phoebe@longlast/together.net</u>

Q. Don't we need bigger help?
from <u>a.giant@least?.net</u>

A. You're right. We need all the governments of the
world to cooperate in solving the climate crisis.
from <u>Ms.Frizzle@the.crossroads</u>

Q. Why does Ms. Frizzle always go on such
weird class trips?
from <u>kids@risk?safety.net</u>

A. That's what I would like to know.
from <u>Arnold@home.sweet.home</u>

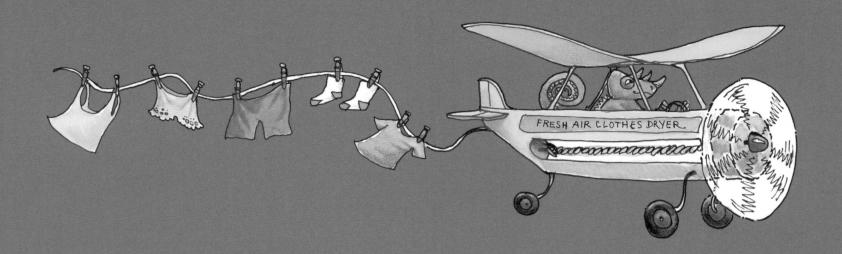